Margaret Caroline Rudd

Authentic Anecdotes of the Life and Transactions of Mrs. Margaret Rudd

Margaret Caroline Rudd

Authentic Anecdotes of the Life and Transactions of Mrs. Margaret Rudd

ISBN/EAN: 9783337155100

Printed in Europe, USA, Canada, Australia, Japan

Cover: Foto ©ninafisch / pixelio.de

More available books at **www.hansebooks.com**

AUTHENTIC ANECDOTES,

OF THE

LIFE AND TRANSACTIONS

OF

MRS. MARGARET RUDD:

Confifting of a Variety of Facts hitherto unknown to the PUBLIC.

ADDRESSED IN

A SERIES OF LETTERS

TO THE

NOW (BY A LATE ACT OF PARLIAMENT)

MISS MARY LOVELL.

Rien n'eft beau, que le vrai, le vrai feul eft aimable
Il droit regner, par tout eft meme dans la fable.
                                            BOILEAU.

VOL. I.

LONDON:

PRINTED FOR J. BEW, No. 28, PATER-
NOSTER-ROW.

MDCCLXXVI.

PREFACE.

AS the contents of the following narrative may appear romantic, or at least improbable, it becomes neceſſary to combat ſuch objection, and to remove every ſuſpicion of this ſort, by appriſing the reader, that all the circumſtances related are ſtrictly true, grounded on facts and the evidence of living witneſſes. The compiler might eaſily have protracted the work to a much greater bulk, from the variety of authentic materials in his poſſeſſion, and which could not be exhibited to

the

the public thro' any other channel: but he has fcrupuloufly fuppreffed many particulars, where there appeared the leaft doubt of their authenticity. He had no other motive in view, but to paint abandoned characters in their true colours, as *objects* of deteftation to their cotemporary age, and as *examples* of abhorrence to the rifing generation. Thus actuated and employed, he has endeavoured to render honeft fervice to his country, to promote the interefts of morality, to guard mankind from future deception and againft thofe crimes by which many have been ruined. Examples have a powerful influence, efpecially on

young

young minds; and when inferences
are properly drawn and precepts
eſtabliſhed, the whole becomes uni-
form and compleat. How far the
following plan will anſwer theſe
purpoſes, is ſubmitted to the judgment of every candid reader.

The female *debauchee* who has ſe-
duced numbers of innocent girls,
and has led aſtray as many married
women, may impudently arrogate
or aſſume to herſelf, the epithets of
amiable and *delicate*——whereas in
reality ſhe is a monſter in iniquity,
and the greateſt peſt to human Society.——Can human language afford
terms too ſevere, or any ſpecies of
ſatire

fatire too poignant againſt a wretch, who has always ſubſiſted on the plunder of individuals and the dilapidations of the public—who has ſupported herſelf in ſcenes of grandeur and diſſipation to the detriment of honeſt tradeſmen, and the ruin of many of her fellow-creatures ? When an artful ſyren has been a principal through a long courſe of the moſt iniquitous practices, why ſhould not ſuch crimes be tranſmited to ſucceeding ages, that innocent poſterity may be upon their guard ? —When a deceitful proſtitute, with the name and figure of a woman, has by a quibble of law, or a concurrence of favourable events, eſcaped

the

the punifhment of criminal juftice
for the prefent——ought not her
criminalities to be recorded that the
young of both fexes may execrate
the vicious example?

Such are the confiderations which
have obtruded the following pages
on the public. And confidering
the numerous publications which
have already appeared on the fame
fubject, but all of them replete with
falfhood and inconfiftencies, it became neceffary as well as a feconda-
ry motive, to publifh a genuine de-
tail.——The prefent plan commen-
ces with an early account of a certain *female*, proceeds in an hiftorical
chain

chain to record such anecdotes and other circumstances as are well attested—and concludes with suggesting what may probably be the final catastrophe of a wicked and profligate woman.

L E T T E R I.

To Mrs. ————

MADAM,

AS I had the honour of an early acquaintance with the gentleman who
had the misfortune to make you—a *wife*;
and as the contents of the following papers are clofely connected with your own
hiftory, it requires the lefs apology for
the freedom of this addrefs. You have
been intimately acquainted with Mrs.
Rudd for feveral years, and a confederate
in various fcenes of proftitution, forgery,

B   and

and intrigue. To extenuate the guilt of your own conduct, you have made many people to believe that this intimacy has been the fole caufe of your ruin. But thofe who know you better, allow this plea to be very confiftent with your ufual tricks of falfhood and deceit, and that you are at leaft her counterpart.

Did that notorious bawd Mrs C—t—n of Jermyn Street introduce Mrs. Rudd to your acquaintance, or you to Mrs. Rudd?—The overtures were certainly made on your part:—for you paid her the firft vifit in Scotland-yard, and foon after had the effrontery to introduce her to your own family as an *immaculate* cha-racter.

It is a difgrace to the annals of any country, as well as an indelible fcandal to human

human nature, that such infamous proftitutes should meet with friendship or protection. And it is a duty and a debt
owing to the community from every honeft individual, to paint such *virtuous*
wives in their true colours, and as a leffon
of abhorrence to the rifing generation.

The affumed names of *Montague, Read,*
and Lady *Catharine Murray,* will inftantly
remind you of your own infamy, as well
as of repeated acts of adultery with different men : and of the horrid confpiracy
between yourfelf and C—l—ns to ruin an
innocent and a much injured man. But
the proceedings in two very refpectable
courts of judicature in this kingdom have
exculpated his character;—while your's
is infamous upon record.

The

The depofitions in Doctors Commons *
prove you to have been callous to all the
feelings of decency, and loft to every
fenfe of fhame. The teftimony of honeft
witneffes will demonftrate that a married
woman, who had a comfortable houfe of
her own, and might have lived in a fphere
of reputation, could wantonly forget the
dignity of human nature, and bid defiance
to the moft facred obligations. And
from an uncommon depravity of difpofition would hire lodgings in different parts
of the town, and frequent them clandeftinely for the purpofes of proftitution, riot
and debauchery. To fanctify her chaftity, an unfeeling mother would fometimes
carry an innocent child to be witnefs of
the

* See the depofitions in a caufe of divorce, Jenkins againft Jenkins.

the moſt ſhocking ſcenes of lewdneſs and
intoxication. Let that wicked nurſe
Anne Suatt deny theſe facts if ſhe can.

It was by the greateſt accident, or rather by the kind interpoſition of providence, that your huſband became acquainted with theſe iniquitous ſcenes and
and vicious practices. And it was with
a becoming ſpirit that he got rid of ſo infernal a connection. But it was your
conſtant cant to miſrepreſent his conduct
to all his acquaintance, who are now perfectly convinced of your wicked arts and
duplicity, and behold the *Fiend* with
pitiable contempt.

Indeed, falſhood and intrigue have
been your diſtinguiſhing characteriſtics
from your infancy; and of this your
friends

friends at Windſor can bear ample teſti-
mony. For the credit of ſociety and the
honour of the ſex, it is devoutly to be
wiſhed that ſuch a character exiſted in
ſpeculation only.

To exhibit your criminalities at large
would prove an endleſs taſk and ſwell this
work into volumes. We ſhall therefore
confine ourſelves to ſuch particulars as
are more immediately connected with the
preſent plan. For your conduct, if tho-
roughly canvaſſed, would appear more
unpardonable to the eye of candour than
that of your colleague. Contemplate for
a moment the ſituation you departed
from, and compare it with your preſent.

When you became acquainted with
Mrs. Rudd, you lived in a very reputable

ble fphere of life; was connected with a
gentleman of induftry and abilities to
fupport your extravagance;—the mother
of a lovely child, and vifited by feveral
families of fafhion and credit. Yet fuch
the frailty of female vanity!—Such the
malignity of your unhappy difpofition,
as wantonly to deviate from the line of
duty! Who then will be furprized to hear
that you are now difcarded by your former acquaintance, and at the mercy of
an unprincipled wretch, and a bankrupt?
This defcription, however humiliating,
difclaims the imputation of falfhood, ma-
levolence or exaggeration;—it is the fim-
ple narrative of truth.—Few anecdotes
will illuftrate the propriety of your private conduct, antecedent to the intimacy
with Mrs. Rudd.

It

It happened at a certain time that the
cellars in your own houſe were plundered
of liquors to a conſiderable value. Upon
this diſcovery your huſband thought it in-
cumbent on him to purſue the neceſſary
ſteps, and to detect, if poſſible, the offen-
ders ; and for this purpoſe carried his
ſervants before a magiſtrate. Your memory has proved treacherous on ſome oc-
caſions, yet it is impoſſible to forget your
own confuſion at this critical juncture.

After a long and tireſome examination,
your own confidential ſervant, to avoid
the confinement of a priſon, gave ſome
account of the ſtolen goods, and acknowledged that her miſtreſs was the—thief.
She further diſcloſed how bountiful you
behaved to different perſons in the ab-
ſence of her maſter ; and at times would
clan-

clandeftinely convey large cargoes of li-
quor and other articles, to places of private affignation in the neighbourhood.
She confeffed withal, that you carried on
a fecret and infamous correfpondence with
feveral men, and made her the innocent
inftrument of intrigue, and of receiving
letters daily by the poft directed to herfelf, but in reality for her *miftrefs*. Need
we to remind you how the magiftrates
and all prefent were fhocked at this extraordinary account ?

After the detection of thefe facts, every
fubfequent part of your conduct fhould
be viewed with an equal eye of jealoufy.
Your hufband was exceedingly hurt by
fuch convincing proofs of your wicked-
nefs and villainy; acquainted your friends
with the particulars of your honefty and

fidelity

fidelity towards him; and was inclined to confign you to the punifhment of criminal juftice. The confideration of having an innocent babe, joined to your own tears of penitence and vows of future difcretion, prevailed on him to overlook your faults for the prefent. You was allowed the privilege of future good behaviour, and to ruminate on your paft mifconduct. But nothing can alter the complexion of human nature. You was born to be the bafeft of your fex, if falfhood and hypocrify, duplicity and intrigue, conftitute an obnoxious character. Your tears of penitence and promifes of amendment lafted but a day.

In fhort, a woman of confummate art and cunning, fond of intrigue, and in love with adulation, can never prove the ami-

able

able or endearing companion. And a woman deftitute of the principles of honour and virtue, is a moft dangerous member of the community. Such is the character now in view.

And notwithftanding the various fchemes recently adopted to miflead the public, and to *wafh the black-a-moor white:* yet the compiler of the following papers, in language unadorned with tropes of rhetorick; or the fubtlety of logical argumentation, refers only to facts and the evidence of living witneffes.

LETTER

L E T T E R II.

M A D A M,

THUS far by way of preface. We shall now advert and investigate another character as extraordinary, but perhaps not more abandoned than your own. The character we mean chiefly to develope, is that of Mrs. Margaret Rudd. A character, which has of late caused much speculation, and various reports about her birth and parentage.

Notwithstanding that much boasted *pedigree*, smuggled with some clandestine view, yet it is a fact, that she is descended from very mean and ignoble parents. Her father, whose name was Youngson, lived

lived as an Apothecary at Lurgan, an obfcure village in the North of Ireland; a perfon of little bufinefs or eminence in his profeffion.

If he had any property, it muft have been inconfiderable, and upon his deceafe fell into the hands of the mortgagee. Her mother was fifter to Mr. John Stewart, who farms his own lands of of fourfcore pounds a-year, and has a contract to fupply the linen manufactory in that part of the kingdom, with potafh. The one died when Mifs Youngfon was an infant; and the other before fhe attained the age of eight years old.

Thus circumftanced, the charge of her education devolved upon her uncle Stewart;—who from motives of charity

charity fent her to fchool at Down-pa-
trick. But our heroine did not continue
there any confiderable time ;—fuch being
her genius at that early period for vici-
ons practices and intrigue, that the parents, one and all threatened to take away
their children, if one immodeft girl was
not immediately difcarded.   It would be
too indelicate to relate the particulars of
a criminal intercourfe that happened between her and one of the fervants belonging to this fchool.   The fact, with all its
aggravating circumftances, is well known
in the town of Downpatrick.

Too many of our boarding fchools
for young ladies, even in the environs of
of this metropolis, are at beft but nur-
feries for vice, and the contagion of bad
examples ;—and where one fcabby fheep
                                                    may

may infect the whole flock. The domestic plan under the inspection of an exemplary parent, is generally the most safe, if not the most accomplished.

From hence our young heroine was removed to Lurgan, to the care of her grandmother Youngson; an old woman not much above the degree of a pauper. Her uncle Stewart having children of his own; and finding after due enquiries, that her behaviour at the school of Downpatrick had proved so vicious and immoral, would by no means admit her into his own house.

While under the inspection of this poor creature, that *turn* for galantry and intrigue, which has since created so much noise and mischief in this metropolis, was

truly

truly confpicuous. For her feeble guardian was perpetually haraffed with compplaints of an uncommon nature; and confequently obliged to have frequent recourfe to difcipline and clofe confinement. However, nothing could tame the wanton difpofition, or cool the irregular fallies of fuch a libidinous girl. Hence fhe elopes with a recruiting fergeant.—But the compaffionate feelings of the commanding officer interpofed, and induced him to fend the young creature back to her difconfolate friends.

Some time after, Lieutenant Rudd happended to come into that part of the kingdom, on the recruiting fervice: and in confequence of ten days acquaintance with Mifs Youngfon, it was his misfortune to make her—a *wife*.

A recital

A recital of the subfequent train of miferies which befel this unhappy man from his conjugal connexion, would excite pity and compaffion in the moft obdurate breaft: and fhould make all future adventurers, extremely cautious how they embark into the fairy land of matrimony, be the external accomplifh-ments of the object as they may——But of this in its proper place.

D   LETTER

LETTER III

MADAM,

HERE our attention is diverted to another object, and a digreffion which we prefume will not be deemed inapplicable. It is fomewhat myfterious, confidering the true account of Mrs. Rudd's birth and parentage in the foregoing letter, by what means or for what purpofe that fpurious *pedigree*, blazoned with the names of fo many illuftrious anceftors, was obtained from Scotland. Without pretending to the gift of prophecy, or the fpirit of divination, we may venture to infer from this inftance, that *pedigrees*, as well as *diplomas*, may be fmuggled from that part of the kingdom on eafy terms.

It

It would be nugatory to difcufs this matter minutely.—But a perfon of affumed confequence, has thought proper to abufe a worthy * Baronet, who had been defrauded of a confiderable property by the artifices of three notorious *fwindlers* ; and for modeftly prefuming to queftion the pretended *pedigree* of the principal. The publication of the fcurrilous writer alluded to, is deferving fome notice and few curfory animadverfions.

The indignant keeper of the *Lyon Records*, in a letter inferted in the Morning Chronicle of October laft, treats his fuperiors with great freedom, and affumes to himfelf airs of *infallibility*. However well verfed Mr. Cummyng may be in the *niceties* of his native dialect, yet

when

* Sir Thomas F——————.

when he attempts to write in the Englifh tongue, his ftyle is neither grammatical nor polite. He undertakes, like his predeceffor of *La Mancha*, to affert the rights of injured innocence: and to exculpate a caluminated individual, while he affumes a total ignorance of her true character. We wifh him to be better informed.

" The abfurdity, fays this man of " confequence, of afking a gentleman " whether a deed is forged or not, when " the fame is diftant four hundred miles " from him, needs no comment. If " there was not a moral certainty that " the original of the letter was *holo-* " *graph* of Sir Thomas, the illiterate " manner in which it is wrote, and the " barbarous inhumanity of the intention

were

" were fufficient to fink it below con-
" tempt. The character of the *Lyon*
" *Office* is fufficiently ·eftablifhed to its
" honour throughout all Europe."

Whatever may be the eftablifhed reputation of the *Lyon Office*, there is a moral
poffibility of its being fometimes liable
to application from impoftors. Was it
impoffible for the gentleman of that *office*
to be impofed upon or deceived in any
circumftance relative to Mrs. Rudd?
Were *they* fo well acquainted with the
particulars of her *cafe* and ftory, as to be
fatisfied of the identity of the character
fhe affumed?——To anfwer thefe inter-
rogatories in the affirmative, would favour of popery and the doctrine of *infal-*
libility.

Let

Let it be granted, that the gentle-men belonging to the *Lyon Office*, are all *men of honour*, and zealous to affert its credit as far as their province or fphere of action can extend. Without depre-ciating their merit or abilities, Mrs. Rudd has impofed on wifer men; and it is much to be feared fhe may again, be-fore providence fhall think proper to con-fign her to that ignominious exit which fhe has long deferved; but by a late fortunate decifion in her favour, has for the prefent efcaped the punifhment of criminal juftice.

The impudence of fome individuals is equal to their ignorance; and the *abfur-dity* of writing civilly to a perfon of *little* Cummyng's confequence, is but too ob-vious from the quotations out of his *bar-*

barous

barous letter. We fhall only obferve, that whatever accefs he might have to perfons of falhion and fortune in Scotland; or opportunities of afcertaining the pedigree of Mrs. Rudd; yet that *pedigree* from a long line of noble and royal anceftors, which fhe has obtruded upon the public, is abfolutely falfe and fpurious. And for the truth of this, we refer the curious to many perfons now living in the north of Ireland, who remember her father a poor Apothecary at Lurgan, and her mother the daughter of an obfcure farmer.

LETTER

MADAM,

WE now refume the thread of our
narrative, where more important
fcenes occur, and our heroine launches into public life.   For in the month of February 1762, the Reverend William Shaw,
minifter of Lurgan, by virtue of a licence,
and with the confent of Mr. John Stewart, Yeoman, married Valentine Rudd,
Lieutenant, and Margaret Youngfon, fpin-
fter, feventeen years old, both of the pa-
rifh of Shankill, in the diocefe of Dro-
more.   This Clergyman, in his letter of
Auguft laft, and now with the editor,
fays exprefsly, that the name of Caroline
was

was not mentiond at that time, nor inserted in his inftructions. And for what purpofes it has been fince adopted, is fubmitted to the conjectures and confideration of the public.

Soon after the aforefaid ceremony was performed, an unfortunate hufband had various reafons to repent of his bargain, as well as ample proofs that his wife was deeply verfed in the fchool of intrigue. Before fhe attained the age of feventeen years, our heroine had given ftriking marks of her future foibles and profligacy.

It need not here be infifted, that a young woman of a volatile difpofition and a tolerable perfon, did not fail of meeting with plenty of admirers who met with

E   no

no material difcouragement. This was
the cafe with our heroine, who conde-
fcended to mingle with all claffes of people previous to her marriage, and every
day brought fome frefh adorer to buoy
up her vanity, and to extol the charms
of her perfon. This circumftance proved very unfavourable to the character of a
wife;—and her conduct in that capacity
was fo barefaced and indecent, that none
of the officers ladies would affociate, or be
feen in the company of Mrs. Rudd.

What a fcene of difappointment and
mortification to a bridegroom, who had
fondly amufed his own fancy with the ac-
quifition of an ineftimable treafure of virtue and conjugal fidelity;—And how
poignant the confideration of having received no addition of fortune from this

freh

frefh engagement, when he perceived the
prodigalities of the partner of his hopes
and expectations !—The very profpect,
even in fpeculation, is terrifying and
dreary to every individual capable of re-
flection.

From this period, an infatuated hufband becomes the heir of mifery and af-
fliction. The regiment to which lieutenant Rudd belonged, was now reduced,
and himfelf to half-pay, on the Irifh e-
ftablifhment, with an accumulated load
of debts contracted by the moft extravagant of women. Thus fituated and perplexed, it was expedient to change the
fcene as foon as poffible, and to afcertain
the beft mode of redrefs.

As he had fome property in Hertfordfhire,

ſhire, his return to England was deemed
the moſt prudent ſtep. Their uncle
Stewart, having a ſlender acquaintance
with Mr. James Adair, of Soho ſquare,
from the contiguity of their lands in the
north of Ireland, preſumed to give them
a letter of recommendation to that gentleman ; and from whence aroſe all the
pretended intereſt and connections with
the family of that name. Hence the
great intimacy with perſons who knew
Mrs. Rudd's *family*, and viſited her frequently. Hence an ingenuity in forming
a valuable acquaintance for various
ſchemes, and the purpoſes of deception.
Hence the generous donations and ſignal
marks of friendſhip impoſed on a credulous
dupe or a knave—And hence a capital train
of forgeries, which convicted the *Perreaus*,
and brought them to the final goal of un-
pitied

pitied ignominy.—But pardon this digreſſion.

Lieutenant Rudd and his wife embarked for England in a Weſt-country trader; and it ſeems at that time to be his plan to ſettle in the neighbourhood of Exeter; from a preſumption, that the neceſſaries of life were more reaſonable in that part of the kingdom, than nearer the metropolis. Here with his half pay and the income of his eſtate he hoped to live comfortably; and it is probable he might have done ſo, had he been bleſſed with a partner of any prudence and frugality.

However, being a native of St. Albans, and having ſome property in that neigh-

neighbourhood, he prefered that spot for the place of residence and retirement. Indeed, his father was a reputable tradesman of that town, and who bestowed on his son a very liberal education; and when he was of proper age, sent him to the University, in order to qualify him for the pulpit.

But the young gentleman not approving this sedentary life, his inclination led him to make choice of another profession; and which proved the means of bringing about the most unhappy connexion that could possibly fall to the share of man. He continued in the country till the summer 1766, when he removed to London, for reasons that shall appear in our next. Notwithstanding the

stri&est

ftricteft frugality and economy on his part, yet he had been obliged to make fome encroachment on his eftate while he lived in the moft private manner and in the retirement of the country.

LETTER

LETTER V.

MADAM,

THE retirement of the country was
by no means a proper fphere for
a woman of Mrs. Rudd's fpirit and profligacy. The metropolis had various
enchantments as well as opportunities
for pleafure and intrigue. It was her
hufband's misfortune to make London
the place of refidence, and to yield to
the importunities of an infolent wife;—
the traces of whofe character, are like
the windings of a labyrinth, dark and
impenetrable. To felect fuch particulars of her conduct, as can be well attefted,

tefted and deferve the notice of the public, is the writer's intention; and to
guard the bulk of mankind from future
deception, his warmeft wifh.

It was in Princefs Street, Cavendifh
Square, and at the houfe of Mr. Marfeilles, a Taylor, that Lieutenant Rudd
took lodgings for his wife and felf when
they removed to town. It fo happened,
that one Cornet Read lodged likewife in
the fame houfe, a young man of genteel
appearance and addrefs; and a proper
objeᴄt for a woman of Mrs. Rudd's paffions, and for the purpofes of intrigue.

Dwelling in the fame houfe, and not
deficient in that affurance which ftamps
the charaᴄteriftic of a native of Hibernia,
he foon contraᴄted an acquaintance with

F   our

our heroine; whofe arts and converfation were too powerful not to attract the heart of a fprightly young fellow. He refolved immediately to lay clofe fiege to a garrifon which his former experience in amorous intrigues, convinced him was not likely to hold out againft a vigorous attack, but would foon furrender to the terms he fhould offer: and it was no long time before he carried his point, and infinuated himfelf into her good graces.

In the month of November, 1776 early in the morning before the family were up, our heroine embraced an opportunity which fhe had been long wifhing for, to make a precipitate retreat with this young officer. But according to the modern mode of elopment, their excurfion was not into Scotland.

The

The Mary-le-bone Coffee Houfe, a fmall diftance from their apartments, was the firft ftage for the completion of their fchemes. Here they continued three days and nights, as a gentleman who had ftole a great fortune, and married her clandeftinely. During this interval, they revelled in high life and in fcenes of luxury, till fome friend of the Cornet came privately to apprize him, that his landlord Marfeilles and the Bailiffs were in clofe purfuit. Direful intelligence this!

However, a plan was well concerted ——- the friend pretends to act the part of a relation to the young lady ; and undertakes to effect a reconciliation, if fhe would return inftantly to her friends. Women are remakable for invention and

fertile

fertile at expedients; and our heroine has the credit of fuggefting this hint and forming the plan. Indeed the fcheme appeared fo plaufible to the people of the houfe, infomuch, that they believed the ftory, and affifted to expedite the re-treat of this friend and the lady in a hackney coach.

Soon after, the Cornet decamps, but without taking leave or making the leaft compenfation to the people of the houfe for their kind and hofpitable reception; for being young and active, he with the agility of a deer top'd the garden wall.

Having pre-concerted where to meet his fair enchantrefs, he immediately fled to the place of appointment, and with all the ardor of impatient love. And

what

what greatly added to the tranfports of joy, was the confideration of having efcaped for the prefent the clutches of thofe fons of violence, the harpies of the law.

Splendid was their manner of living for fome time at Richmond and Green-wich, and elfewhere, on the dilapidations of the public, and the plunder of indi-viduals. At length the moft private and retired fituation became abfolutely necef-fary; and after various enquiries as well as due deliberation, Mr. Crofby's Tripe Shop, at Ratcliff-crofs, was agreed upon as the moft convenient fpot. Here they lived upwards of four months in a wick-ed and adulterous manner; and our heroine feemed in a fair way for a while to honour her paramour with a living pledge

pledge of their commerce and amours, but in the event it proved abortive.

No finances will fuffice for the prodigalities of an abandoned woman; and Cornet Read was now fenfible of this, notwithftanding the many unwarrantable fteps which he purfued, even by riding out late in the evenings, in order to preferve the connexion, and was at laft obliged to fly his country, to avoid the horrors and confinement of a prifon.

Many people loft confiderable fums by the imprudent conduct of this young officer, particularly Mr. Marfeilles the Taylor. And we fhall fee by and by, whofe lot it was to be arrefted, and to defray the expences of the long and adulterous correfpondence at the Tripe Shop in Ratcliff.

LETTER

LETTER VI.

MADAM,

IT is now time to return to Lieutenant Rudd, who, after the moſt aſſiduous enquiries could not find or trace his wife; but concluded that ſhe was gone to Ireland with Cornet Read. Being very unhappy in his own mind, and in want of money, he applies to one Lary in Park Street, and ſells to him what few things and articles of apparel his wife had left.

However, he at length received an explicit account of his wife as well as of

the

the infamous tranfactions during the period of her elopement ; for to his forrow
many perfons were now in fearch of him
for the payment of confiderable debts
contracted by his wife, and feveral actions
commenced againft an unfortunate hufband.

Having learnt where his wife cohabited with her galant, the injured hufband repaired directly to the fpot ; but
he was not permitted to fee her. He
afterwards repeated his vifits to the
fame place, but it was all in vain ; and
he almoft defpaired, though he was determined to exert his utmoft endeavours,
to reclaim a woman for whom he had fo
great a regard.

On the twenty-fixth of February 1767,
Mr.

Mr. Rudd, in return for his great anxiety and endeavours to reclaim an abandoned woman, was arrested at the request and by the direction of his wife, and sent to the Poultry. On the 14th of the enfuing month, for want of bail, he was removed on a writ of *habeas corpus* to the King's Bench prison; where he remained till the 7th of May, when he was difcharged by a rule of court on fpecial bail.

This cafe is fingularly cruel and oppreffive; and feems to argue a degree of latitude in the laws of this country, which give a *wife* an unlimited, if not an improper power. Our eminent fages of the law, and perfons of benevolence, would render honeft fervice to their country by taking this matter into immediate con-

G   fideration,

fideration, and confequently prove the means of faving individuals from deftruction.

Lieutenant Rudd thought it extremely hard and cruel to be imprifoned for debts contracted by his wife, while fhe and her gallant lived together in a wicked and adulterous manner: but although he had experienced his wife's ungenerous treatment, and in all probability might have caft the plantiff if it had come to a trial, as *Read* was the proper perfon who ought to have paid the debt, yet fo tender was Lieutenant Rudd of his wife's reputation, that rather than expofe her in a court of judicature, he compounded the matter, and thus quietly put an end to it.

Soon

Soon after his enlargement and the in-
conveniencies of a prifon, Mr. Rudd
found it neceffary to take fhelter at Mrs.
Kennedy's, in the verge of the court—
a multiplicity of frefh actions being out
againft him on account of his wife. What
fituation can be conceived fo deplorable
as that of this perfecuted and diftreffed
hufband?—And what was to be done to
extricate himfelf from fuch a load of
heavy calamities?—He had now no alternative, but to fell his patrimony in
Hertfordfhire, difcharge the debts, and
fue for a divorce from the worft and moft
abandoned of women.

Accordingly application was made to
Mr. Blake, Attorney of Effex Street,
and alfo to a proctor in the commons, in
order

order to accomplish these salutary pur-
poses. But it must *here* be observed,
that previous to these steps, and in perfect
confistence with the consummate villany
of the bafeft of her fex, Lieutenant Rudd,
while in prifon, had been ferved with a
citation from the Commons for cruelty
and adultery. B—g—ve of infamous
memory, returned a citation in behalf of
Margaret, and not *Caroline*, Rudd. Tor-
riano appeared for Valentine Rudd, cited
to libel ;—continued to next term:——
but no libel was given by Margaret Rudd
or her proctor.

Tho' Lieutenant Rudd ardently wifhed for a divorce and a final releafe from
his infernal connexion; yet as Captain
Read could not be ferved with the regular
procefs to maintain an action for criminal
convlerfa-

converfation, or for want of evidence to afcertain facts, it did not take place. Perhaps it might not correfpond at this period with Lieutenat Rudd's circumftances to proceed with fuccefs in fo expenfive an undertaking.

The neceffary procefs to obtain a divorce in this country is almoft endlefs, as well as attended with a prodigious expence; and as matters ftand at prefent, the due confideration of this fubject feems loudly to demand the attention of the Legiflature. In other countries, the mode of proceeding in fuch cafes is much eafier and more expeditious; and if marriage is an human inftitution, why fhould not human laws provide an eafy remedy to diffolve it, whenever the obligation of the covenant becomes forfeited by either party.

However,

However, the attorney was more fuc-
cefsful with regard to the eftate at St.
Alban's, which he fold; and Lieutenant
Rudd found himfelf poffeffed of a confiderable fum of money, which enabled
him to difcharge the large debt contracted at the tripe fhop, in Ratcliff-crofs,
and many others.

LETTER

LETTER VII.

MADAM,

DURING the confinement of the husband in prison, our heroine had an opportunity to form various connexions, and some useful ones; and though she received very handsome presents almost every day, yet her extravagance would never keep within bounds. But her principal aim, as well as particular boast, was the peculiar method of rendering feeble and aged lovers exceedingly enamoured of her. The artful lady failed not to make a proper use of such doating admirers;——she caressed, fondled,

and

and exerted all the craft of woman to gain an entire predominancy.

Many inſtances of this nature will occur in the courſe of this narrative. And as her temper and genius never approved of an inactive ſtate of life, it happened on a time, that ſhe connected herſelf with a notorious gang of *Swindlers*, and among whom ſhe bore a principal character; being repreſented to credulous tradeſmen as a lady of great fortune, the natural daughter of the Pretender, and grandchild of Lord Dundee. This mode of life brought in for a while large revenues, till unfortunately for her, the clan was broke, and numbers fell into the hands of juſtice.

As the Pretender's daughter had been

been fo extremely ferviceable in carrying
on this bufinefs, it is no wonder that
ftrict fearch was made after her ladyfhip,
but it was all in vain. Whether at this
juncture, or when Captain Read abfconded from Ratcliff, and that infamous connexion ceafed for the prefent, yet it is
an undoubted fact, that our heroine
came to lodge at an Oil Shop in St.
Martin's Lane.

Here we are furnifhed with an anecdote worthy the obfervation of the public, and which muft convince every candid reader of her early proficiency in the
arts of forgery and deceit. Being rather
bare of cloaths, as well as deftitute of
money, her landlady introduced her to
the fhop of Mr. Hogard, Haberdafher,
in Long Acre, who trufted her with

H   goods

goods to the value of four guineas, on
the recommendation of his neighbour.

A woman hackneyed in all the ways
of vice and proſtitution, ſeldom wants
effrontery to promote any ſcheme of villainy or fraud. Soon after the firſt interview, ſhe again repaired to the ſame
ſhop, with a larger demand for goods :—
but the honeſt tradeſman, judging from
appearances, that ſhe muſt be a woman
of the town, refuſed to comply with ſo
extraordinary a requeſt. And in juſtice
to himſelf obſerved, that it was his inva-
riable rule never to truſt perſons of her
complexion with goods to any large
amount.

Neither daunted nor diſappointed at
this refuſal, ſhe produced a note for one
hundred

hundred pounds, payable thirty days after date; affured Mr. *Hogard*, that fhe was a lady of family and fortune; and confequently above the neceffity of being obliged to him for credit, or for any other favour in a tradefman's power. In fhort, fhe only defired him to difcount the note, pay his own bill, and give her the balance.

Mr. *Hogard* fomewhat furprifed, and rather confounded at fo unexpected an explanation, defired her to leave the note, and he would prepare the goods and fend them agreeably to the order. But on confulting his men of bufinefs, they all agreed that the note was a grofs forgery —becaufe the names of the drawer, accepter and endorfer, were wrote by one and the fame hand.

After

After the detection of this fact, every subsequent part of her conduct should be viewed and investigated with an equal eye of jealousy. Mr *Hogard* omitted no pains to trace the drawer, accepter and indorser; but all in vain. And though the note was due in the month of May, yet he kept it in his possession till the latter end of August following, when he delivered it up into the hands of Lieutenant Rudd, at Mr. Thompson's, in Scotland Yard, and was paid his debt in full.

This anecdote exhibits strong circumstances to believe that this note for one hundred pounds was forged; and that a certain *female* was an early adept in the most iniquitous practices. Will the many volunteers inlisted in the service of

a bad

a bad caufe, now applaud this paragon
of confcious innocence, and acquit her
of every criminal intention ?—Will the
tongue of folly or credulity pretend to
fay, that fhe did not fign thofe bonds
which convicted the Perreaus, and
brought them to an ignominious death ?

The texture of her delicate feelings muft
be fhocked at the recollection of an anecdote which fhe fondly imagined had been
buried in oblivion——And her *fublimity
of foul added to a refinement of fentiment,*
muft be fatisfied of the authenticity of
the fact, by a reference to the party who
is now alive.

L E T T E R VIII.

NOtwithſtanding the comfortable ſum
of money as mentioned in a former letter, and which an unfortunate
and perſecuted huſband had received from
the ſale of his eſtate; yet there was a certain proſpect of its being ſoon expended
by the continual demands on account of
his wife. It muſt be a very cruel as well
as an unpleaſant taſk for a man of feel-
ing, to part with thoſe paternal acres ac-
quired by the induſtry of honeſt anceſ-
tors—*And* to be under an abſolute neceſſity of appropriating their whole value
to diſcharge debts wantonly contracted

by

by the prodigalities of an abandoned proftitute, is a confideration extremely mortifying. Yet fuch was the cafe of the
unfortunate man more immediately connected with the thread of our narrative.

If there is a curfe entailed upon man
and irremediable this fide of the grave, it
is *that* of being connected with a vicious,
artful, and extravagant wife. All other
misfortunes are furmountable in time,
and may be removed by a concurrence of
fortunate events—while this *evil* admits
of no releafe or alleviation but from the
hand of death.

Thrice happy they who have never
felt the afflictions, or experienced the
wretchednefs of fuch a condition! And
it is to be wifhed for the honour of hu-
manity

manity, and the peace of individuals, that many of our modern *wives* had never been born. For they feem to have entered into the moft facred obligations, and to have coveted the name of *wife*, only as a cloak for profligacy and licentiouf-nefs, or a fanction for fcenes of darknefs and iniquity. The characters in view juftify thefe melancholy reflections, as will more fully appear in the profecution of our plan : and fhould prove a leffon to youth how cautious they ought to be from facrificing their happinefs at the fhrine of external accomplifhments, fortune or appearances.

Thefe obfervations were natural to the unfortunate hufband now confined to his lodgings in the verge of the court, and who dared not to venture abroad for certain

tain reafons, except on *one* day in the week. He had, nevertherthelefs, the generofity to hire lodgings in the neighbourhood for an ungrateful wife, and to be refponfible for a reafonable maintenance. Her former gallant was become invifible, or had abfconded on account of debts and other mifdemeanours;—it was therefore probable that fo infamous an attachment would entirely fubfide.

From repeated affurances of her contrition and amendment, as well as the interpofition of friends, Mr. Rudd was almoft prevailed upon to forgive and cohabit with his wife. And about this time, and for this purpofe, a treaty was actually fet on foot by their refpective friends, and a perfect reconciliation would have enfued, had the promifes on her part

I proved

proved fincere. All former foibles would
have been buried in oblivion, the remain-
der of their lives might have paffed happy and uninterrupted, their names efcaped public cenfure, and recent fcenes of
villainy and bloodfhed precluded.

But nothing can reclaim an abandoned
woman, or at leaft *one* of our heroine's
complexion. An old acquaintance being
juft arrived from abroad, and on his
rout for Ireland to take poffeffion of a
confiderable eftate, which had devolved
to him on the deceafe of an uncle, immediately difpatched his emiffaries to apprize his fair enchantrefs of the joyous
event.

Upon the receipt of thefe welcome tid-
ings her former fondnefs for the lover
awak-

awakened with redoubled ardour; every refolution of amendment inftantly forfook her, and the fair inconftant prepared for a fecond elopement. In fhort, away fhe hurried in a poft chaife, and carried with her as a companion an innocent young girl, who fell a victim to the moft diabolical artifices and intrigue.—But *here* the rules of decency and other confiderations oblige us to draw a veil, and to omit the particulars of a barbarous tranfaction.

It feems that a regular correfpondence had fubfifted between our heroine and this gallant ever fince his flight from the tripe fhop at Ratcliff highway. Lieutenant Rudd by fome means was apprized of this correfpondence, and on going to his wife's lodgings he had the curiofity to examine the drawers, where he found a very curious collection of a-morous epiftles. This event diftreffed the delicacy of Mrs. Rudd extremely; and fhe afterwards endeavoured, by every artifice as well as by promifes of fpeedy preferment, to feduce an officer who lodg-ed in the fime houfe with her hufband in the verge of the court, to recover thefe precious manufcripts at any rate. But fuch an attempt was impracticable; the hufband having had the precaution to lodge them in proper hands.

It is reafonable to fuppofe that this laft elopement would break off the intended reconciliation with her hufband—wean him of every fpark of affection, and roufe his indignation againft fo many repeated acts of falfhood and infidelity to the mar-riage

riage bed. However, after ftaying out two days and nights, the innocent lady returned with as perfect compofure as if fhe had only been upon a trifling vifit. It was in vain fhe fued for an interview with her hufband, who refufed to fee her, and was determined not to maintain a woman fo abandoned, and who purfued every method to bring both herfelf and him into difgrace. Accordingly he difcharged the debts at the houfe from whence fhe laft eloped, and warned the people in writing, to truft his wife no longer.

Moreover, he caufed an advertifement to be inferted in the daily advertifer of the 8th of November 1767, in the following words——" Whereas Magaret, wife of Valentine Rudd, gentleman, has with-

withdrawn herſelf from her huſband, this is therefore to caution all perſons a-gainſt giving her credit on her huſband's account, as he will not pay any debts ſhe contracts."

Let the deluded multitude now pity this fair innocent!—Let her advocates candidly exculpate her conduct, if they can! Let the myriads of volunteers en-liſted in her ſervice plead the *texture of her delicate feelings*; and inſiſt that theſe harmleſs excurſions were perfectly con-ſiſtent with a *ſublimity of ſoul added to a refinement of ſentiment.*

LETTER IX.

MADAM,

WHEN our heroine returned from the laſt excurſion, her finances, it ſeems, were at a low ebb; and it was expedient that her gallant ſhould proſecute his route to Ireland and take poſſeſſion of his uncle's eſtate. However poignant the pangs of parting from his fair enchantreſs might be, yet he was under the indiſpenſable neceſſity of leaving her for the preſent, and without thoſe pecuniary conſiderations requiſite to ſupport a woman above indigence and diſtreſs.

Thus abandoned and forlorn, the fair in-

inconftant was obliged to fue for a night's lodging at the houfe from whence fhe had laft eloped. The people there had the compaffion to accommodate the petitioner for a night; and next morning they waited on her hufband, who lived privately in the verge of the court, in order to work on his good nature and forgiving temper, and to negotiate terms of accommodation in behalf of the wife.

But the injured hufband, fenfible of repeated wrongs, of the moft ungenerous treatment, and roufed with indignation, pofitively refufed to liften to any propofals;—infifted that he would not be refponfible for future debts or expence; and that they ought by no means to harbour and countenance fuch a foul adultrefs.

Though

Though her favourite gallant was gone to Ireland on bufinefs of fome confequence and emolument to himfelf, yet fuch the powers of attraction, and the fafcinating arts of a certain forcerefs!—and fuch his own infatuated attachment to her charms!—that this fon of Mars returned in a fhort time, and about this critical juncture arrived in the metropolis to alleviate the diftreffes of our heroine.

As foon as he had accommodated himfelf with lodgings at Mrs. Macab's in Frith Street Soho, and where for prudential motives he affumed the name of Captain *Shee*, he ftrolled in fearch of his Duenna. Few nights after his arrival, and as he was patroling the ftreets, he accidentally met with the object of his wifhes and ufhered her to the new apartments.

K   This

This is an event which has not hitherto tranfpired to many, and what our heroine has had the effrontery to deny, tho'.
the connexion is well known to perfons
of undoubted veracity ;—efpecially to
Courtoy the hair dreffer and deputies,
who at this period and in their vocation
waited on Mr. and Mrs. *Shee.* Our heroine happens to be particularly diftin-
guifhed by a remarkable * fcar in a certain place near the face, and which was
received in confequence of unlawful adventures —perhaps in a fit jealoufy, and
for infidelity to the marriage bed. It
would have been fortunate for the community, as well as for the welfare of individuals, if providence had fo ordered
mat-

* Jametty, an Italian Frifeur knows Mrs. Rudd
and Mrs. Shee to be one and the fame perfon by a
fcar on her neck.

matters, and that this wound had proved effectual.

Captain *Shee* and lady lived at thefe a-partments in Frith Street for fome months in great luxury and feftivity, and on a prefumption of being perfons of great affluence and property in Ireland. But the fmiles of fortune are fickle and precarious, and human happinefs is ever liable to cafualties or diminution.—A continual fcene of gaity and extravagance had made a great encroachment on the Captain's finances and revenues; and now his neceffities compelled him to be troublefome to his friends, and frequently to folicit a fupply.

Thus at length they found his retreat as well as his mode of living; and having

ing a particular regard for his father, an alderman of Dublin, they fent him an explicit account of his fon's fituation— of having affumed a new name, and the infamous connexion with a married wo- man—and that he was in the high road to deftruction both of body and foul.

The alderman, full of parental tender- nefs and affection, was exceedingly fhock- ed at the receipt of this difagreeable in- telligence, and extremely alarmed at the difappointment of felicity to an aged pa- rent and his family. Wifhing to pre- vent, if poffible, the total ruin of his fon, the alderman embarked for England with the utmoft anxiety and expedition, and when he reached the metropolis, was advifed to ftop at Foreft's coffee houfe, Charing

Charing crofs, and there accommodated with lodgings.

Having made the neceffary enquiries how to find and where to fee his fon, he directed his courfe one morning to Macab's in Frith Street, where he furprized Mr. and Mrs. *Shee* in bed together; and was made to underftand that this *virtuous* pair had cohabited there for fome time.

The alderman, as the firft preliminary towards a reconciliation with his fon, infifted that the lady fhould be inftantly difcarded, and which was readily agreed. Probably, this proved the laft interview with this diffipated young officer, as well as the final period to their wicked and illicit amours. The amount of debts contracted during this intercourfe was aftonifhing;

niſhing; and perhaps the impoveriſhed
ſtate of his finances, together with the
daily apprehenſion and horrors of a priſon, was the principal conſideration that
induced him ſo readily to comply with
the requeſt and remonſtrances of a tender parent.

The alderman being determined that
the ſon of his hopes and induſtry ſhould
no longer ſtay in London, or in the
neighbourhood of a fatal enchantreſs,
carried him over to Dublin, after paying
his debts. Whether from motives of
ſhame, or for want of principle, he did
not diſcloſe one capital debt at this time
to the father.

But we ſhall now bid a final *adieu* to
this profligate young man, who died in
prifon

prifon at Dublin three hundred pounds
in debt to Marfeilles the taylor; and
who in a great meafure owed his ruin to
the fafcinating powers of Mrs. Rudd.
But her arts have fent many, befides
him, on an untimely voyage for the cape
of *good hope.*

LETTER

LETTER X.

MADAM,

TO be difcarded in fo abrupt a manner as mentioned in our laft, and
without that degree of ceremony due to
the foftnefs of the fex, was a confideration extremely mortifying to a lady of
our heroine's confequence and refined
pretenfions. The furprife occafioned by
the arrival of an unexpected vifitor was
truly affecting, and caufed much diftrefs
as well as confufion to delicate feelings,
added to a fublimity of foul—And this
event made our heroine once more to
wander a citizen of the Streets, and to
rely on her own ingenuity, and the chapter of accidents for fupport.

At

At length, by fome means or other, fhe ftumbled at the door of one Mr. Hyde, who then kept a houfe in Northumberland Street, in the Strand; and where fhe procured a recommendation to lodge and board, under a pretence of being the wife of a gentleman of character, and a man of fortune. The landlord being thus deceived in refpect to *her* circumftances and *his* own expectations, chearfully entrufted his gueft with board and lodging, and doubted not of being honeftly paid fome time or other.

But having no vifible means of fubfiftence, except the conftant practice of going out in the dufk of the evenings to walk the ftreets, the landlord was juftly alarmed, became clamorous and uneafy on various accounts. It feems

L   that

that he had now been undeceived by the kindnefs of a friend or the reprefentations of a neighbour, who apprized him, that his gueft lived apart from her hufband, as plainly appeared from the contents of a public advertifement exhibited for his perufal.

After ocular demonftration of his own credulity, and the impofition on her part, he immediately repaired to Mrs. Kennedy's, in the verge of the court, and applied to an unfortunate hufband for the payment of a confiderable bill, for lodging and board to his wife.

But the perfecuted hufband refufed payment for the prefent—remonftrated againft the legality of the debt—fhewed him the advertifement as quoted in a

former

former letter, and fet him at defiance. Notwithftanding this expoftulation, the landlord fuffered his gueft to continue at his houfe for fome time longer, and took another mode of application to the hufband for fatisfaction to his demand.

The defendant wifhing to decline, if poffible, the expences of the law as well as the iffue of a trial, offered to compound the matter, and to pay at the rate of a guinea a week, in full proportion to his income, and rather more than his perplexed circumftances could afford. But this propofal, though highly legal, and altogether reafonable, was rejected as not fatisfactory to the plantiff.

Proceedings were then commenced at the fuit of Hyde, and a trial enfued in
the

the firft fittings after Eafter term 1768, when Sollicitor General Dunning, and Mr. Mansfield, were the counfel for the defendant.

The queftion to be tried—what the plaintiff ought to recover of the defendant for the expences of his wife who had eloped from him, and was well known by the plaintiff to live feparate from him. And here it is to be obferved, that if the defendant, under the circumftances of the cafe, was obliged to maintain his wife at all, it could only be in a reafonable way, and according to his degree and eftate.

It is alfo prefumed, that the money tender'd in court at the rate of a guinea a week, was at all events a full fatisfaction

tion to the plaintiff, for the board and lodging of Mrs. Rudd, for she lodged in his two pair of ftairs ; and the manner of the plaintiff's living was very mean, and fhe found her own tea, fugar, wine, coals and candles.

It feems to be a fettled rule of law, that the neceffaries fupplied a wife, whilft fhe lives feparate from the hufband, fhould be only neceffary and convenient for the hufband's eftate as well as degree.

How is it in the prefent cafe?—The hufband, Mr. Rudd, is a Lieutenant on half pay on the Irifh eftablifhment, which produces him thirty-two pounds a year; and he has the intereft of about fixteen hundred pounds, the money left from

the

the fale of his eftate, which produces at a current calculation fixty pounds annually.

So that his whole income is but ninety fix pounds a year, and if obliged to pay one pound eleven fhillings and fixpence a week, the plaintiff's charge for his wife's board and maintenance, he would have nothing left for himfelf to live on, without breaking in upon the principal of his little fortune. Wherefore, it was hoped that the court and jury would confider the money tendered into court, as an ample fatisfaction for the plaintiff's demand, confidering the defendant's degree and eftate.

To prove the manner of Mrs. Rudd's living at her former lodgings, what fhe

paid

paid a week, and that fhe lived apart from her hufband, and alfo that the plaintiff was made acquainted with Mrs. Rudd's fituation, a witnefs was called, and on oath gave fatisfaction to the court with regard to thefe facts.

When the plaintiff took her in, and that he trufted her at his peril, and knew of the advertifement being inferted by the defendant, and that a guinea a week was an ample fatisfaction to the plaintiff, another witnefs was called, and depofed accordingly.

To prove that the defendant's wife eloped from her laft lodgings, previous to her coming to the plaintiff's houfe, and ftayed out two nights—to prove the poor manner of Mrs. Rudd's living in
the

the plaintiff's family—and to prove the
defendant's circumftances and eftate,
other reputable witneffes were called, and
gave fatisfaction to the court with relation to every and all fuch particulars.

LETTER

L E T T E R   XI.

MADAM,

OUR laſt concluded with ſome particulars of the cauſe between Hyde
and Rudd; and to prove the authenticity of our aſſertions, we alſo gave an
abſtract of the brief of one of the counſel.
Perhaps, it may not be improper here
to inſert a true copy of the affidavit of
Valentine Rudd, and which may tend to
illuſtrate or corroborate the contents of
ſome of the preceding letters.

Eaſter Term, 26th April, 1768. *Firſt
ſitting at* Weſtminſter-hall.

" Valentine Rudd, of the pariſh of St.
M   Martin

Martin 'in the Fields, in the liberty of
Weſtminſter, and county of Middleſex,
Gentleman, maketh oath, and ſaith, that
he was a Lieutenant in the army in Ireland in the year 1762, and during that
time, he this deponent, at Lurgan, in
the county of Armagh, became acquainted with Margaret Youngſon, and was
married to her there, according to the
rites and ceremonies of the Church of
England, by the Curate of that place,
by licence, and by the conſent of her
uncle Mr. John Stewart, who was her
guardian, and gave her in name to this
deponent. And this deponent ſaith, that
he lived with his ſaid wife in Ireland, till
the concluſion of the laſt war, when the
regiment to which this deponent belonged was reduced, and this deponent was
put upon half pay; and thereupon this
deponent

deponent came into England with his said
wife, in order to manage and transact
this deponent's own affairs, he being intitled to a considerable freehold and copy-
hold estate in the county of Hertford,
where this deponent was born, and which
estate this deponent received the rents of;
and therewith, and with his halfpay,
continued to live with, and maintain his
said wife in a comfortable manner, from
the time of his coming into England,
which was in or about the year 1763, to
the time of her acquaintance with the
said defendant Benjamin Bowen Read, in
the year 1768; and during that time,
this deponent and his wife lived in a very
harmonious and affectionate manner, this
deponent having no ground to suspect her
being any way unfaithful to him. And
this deponent saith, that in the summer

of

of the year 1766, he and his said wife went to lodge at the house of one Marseilles a Taylor, in Princes Street, Cavendish Square, in the first floor. And soon after they went to lodge there, the said defendant, Benjamin Bowen Read, came to lodge there likewise in the second floor, and by that means the said defendant became acquainted with this deponent and his said wife ; and he the said defendant then passed for a young gentleman, intitled to a confiderable estate ; and this deponent and the said Read grew very intimate together, and in the month of October or November 1766, the said Read, left his said lodgings in Princes Street aforesaid, but this deponent had not then suspected that there was any intrigue between the said Read, and his,

this

this deponent's said wife. And this deponent saith, that a very short time after the said Read went away, a letter from him was brought to this deponent's said wife, at which this deponent expressed some surprise and anger, and by means thereof a slight quarrel ensued between this deponent and his said wife, and she thereupon refused to lie with this deponent that night, and the next morning she got up before the other people in the house, and went away and left this deponent, and co-habited, as this deponent afterwards found, with the said defendant, Read, and lived with him at one Bradshaw's, a Surgeon and Apothecary, at Ratcliff Highway, where this deponent went to enquire after her, but this deponent was not permitted to see her, though

she

she was then in the house with the said
Read. And this deponent saith, that
his said wife continued to co-habit with
the said Read, as this defendant verily
believed, and to secrete herself from this
deponent till the month of March last,
when the said Read went abroad, as was
given out by this deponent's said wife:
and this deponent was soon afterwards
arrested for the board and lodging of his
said wife, during part of the time she so
lived away from this deponent. And
this deponent saith, that he hath not till
lately been able to obtain proper evi-
dences of facts to maintain an action
against the said Read, for criminal con-
versation with this deponent's said wife.
And this deponent saith, that he hath
been informed and believes, that the said
Read is now in England. But this deponent

ponent faith, that if he, this deponent,
was to bring an action againft him, the
faid Read, and ferve him with a copy of
procefs, only with holding him to bail,
he this deponent would lofe the benefit
and effect of fuch action, as this deponent verily believes. For this deponent
faith, that he believes that the faid Read,
would, upon his being ferved with a
procefs, go abroad out of this kingdom;
for he, the faid Read, is an Irifhman by
birth, as this deponent hath heard and
believes; and his property, which is
confiderable, as this deponent hath heard,
lies in that kingdom, he having no property here, as this deponent believes.
And this deponent faith, he hath heard
and been informed, that the faid Read
attained the age of 25 years, in October
laft, and that therefrom he became in-

titled

titled to the poffeffion of a confiderable
eftate in Ireland, of the yearly value of
two thoufand pounds, or fome fuch large
fum of money."

The contents of this affidavit feem to
elucidate many particulars, and exactly
to correfpond with the feveral facts hitherto infifted on in the courfe of our
narrative. The period of their coming
to England is confirmed ; and the elopement from Princes Street is alfo acknowledged.

The other circumftances and anecdotes intervened from November 1766,
to the date of the foregoing affidavit in
the year 1768, when our heroine lived
altogether feparate from her hufband,
and when the defendant Read could not

be

be found —— having fecreted himfelf for fome time, under the affumed name of Captain *Shee*; or had juft failed for Ireland, in company with his father, as mentioned in a former letter.

N   LETTER

L E T T E R   XII.

MADAM,

OUR heroine ftill continued her former plan of life; ftill contracted
large debts, and ftill left her hufband to
pay for them.   No wonder that thefe
continual drains and repeated demands
foon exhaufted the principal remaining
from the fale of his patrimony and fmall
eftate.   The perfecuted hufband found
himfelf again arrefted, and detainers lodged againft him at the fuit of different cre-
ditors whom he never faw ; and that it
was impoffible once more to avoid or ef-
cape the confinement of a prifon.   His
fituation was truly pitiable as well as melancholy.

It

It feems that the wife had concerted a
plan to compel a reconciliation with her
hufband, notwithftanding repeated inftances of elopement and mifconduct; but
how fhe could imagine that he would a-
gain become a dupe to her infinuating
methods, is wonderful! And how a
man of fpirit could liften to any propofals or terms of reconciliation with fo a-
bandoned a wife, is ftill more aftonifhing! Perhaps, his diftreffes and the dif-
ficulties wherein her fchemes had invol-
ved him, admitted of no other alternative.

However, being perpetually haraffed
with debts, law fuits and arrefts, and a
variety of other troubles on account of
his wife, the unfortunate hufband thought
it high time that matters fhould be fettled

on

on fome permanent plan. With this view and about this time, their refpective friends interpofed, held feveral conferences, and a treaty was fet on foot, either for a reconciliation or a total feparation on equitable terms.

During this negotiation our heroine perfonally waited on her hufband in the verge of the court; implored his forgivenefs and made folemn vows of amendment, of conjugal fidelity and attachment for the future. There is no accounting for the bewitching powers and the flattering hypocrify of an artful fyren. Heathen writers abound with inftances in confirmation of this affertion; and we read in facred fong how the wifeft men have been impofed upon and became victims to the wiles and craft of a woman.

The

The doating hufband has frequently repented of his own credulity, as well as the conviction of his own better judgment and experience. The perfon more immediately in view ftill retaining a degree of fondnefs for the moft ungrateful woman, or at leaft not able to withftand her ufual arts of falfhood and duplicity, gave credit to the fincerity of her proteftations — a reconciliation took place, and they came to live together at Mr. Thompfon's in Scotland yard.

After fo many inftances of ill-ufage and infidelity to the marriage bed—of debts wantonly contracted, law-fuits, arrefts, and imprifonment, how could any hufband entertain the moft diftant idea, or bear the thoughts of a reconciliation with fuch an abandoned wife?—A man

of

of refentment and proper feelings would have embraced any alternative, rather than cohabit with fo foul an adultrefs.

Her fubfequent conduct and demeanour, as will foon appear, merited no returns of fondnefs or indulgence, and the deluded hufband had ample caufe to repent of his own credulity and attachment. For her tears of penitence and promifes to reclaim, lafted but a day; they were only meant as a cloak of deception, and to enable her the more eafily to effect her own purpofes and fchemes of intrigue. No long time after this reconciliation, a diftreffed hufband was heard to exclaim againft his wife to the following effect.

" Oh! Peggy, Peggy, you have now forgot that I fent you back to your grand-

grandmother at Lurgan, and took no advantage of your youth or indifcretion,
though you followed me twenty miles.
You have alfo forgot that I married you
in an unguarded hour—that 1 have fold
my patrimony to pay your debts and in-
dulge your extravagance—that I have
been always partial to your foibles and
levities—that my behaviour towards you
was tender and affectionate, and could
have kiffed the ground whereon you trod.
Surely ! I merit better treatment at your
hands in this my deep diftrefs, O moft
ungrateful of women !"

How could an unfeeling *wretch* turn a
deaf ear to this artlefs tale, and to the ur-
gent neceffities of the man fhe had ruined ? Should any perfon doubt the reality of thefe complaints, or the diftrefs of
the

the supplicant, we wish to refer them
for further satisfaction to the landlady in
Buckingham court, and whose name has
been repeatedly mentioned. And we shall
see by and bye in what scenes of plenty
our heroine revelled, when the above
mentioned soliloquy was extorted from
the most unfortunate husband.

LETTER

LETTER XIII.

MADAM,

SOON after the reconciliation mentioned in our laft, they came to lodge
in the neighbourhood of Grofvenor fquare,
and where your intimacy with our heroine
commenced.—From this period you and
Mrs. Rudd became infeparable compa-
nions and confederate in various fcenes
of vice, to the degradation of the fex—
the ruin of your refpective hufbands, and
the annoyance of all your neighbours.

A married woman is the guardian of
her hufband's honour, and fhould be
extremely cautious what company fhe
keeps, and what connexions fhe ought to

O   make.

make. If not ſtrictly virtuous herſelf, at
leaſt jealous to keep up appearances.
Verſed from your infancy in the ſchool
of levity and intrigue, you had not the
precaution to preſerve an honourable engagement. Though you have lately
made ſome perſons to believe, that your
own ruin is entirely owing to an intimacy
with Mrs. Rudd ; yet we who know you
better, allow you to be at leaſt her counterpart.

The lodgings at Mrs. Cranſton's in
Park Street were common for the reception of your ſeveral gallants, and for the
purpoſes of riot, proſtitution and intrigue. Perhaps, ſome of the moſt abandoned women within the purlieus of Covent garden, would bluſh at the recital
of the infamous correſpondence and connexions

nexions in this houfe.—But here the
rules of decency oblige us to ftop.

Lieutenant Rudd foon found caufe to
repent of his own credulity, as well as of
fondnefs for his wife. He had now convincing proofs what flender credit is due
to the moft folemn proteftations from an
artful and profligate woman. It was his
misfortune about this time, as you well
remember, to be confined to a bed of
ficknefs, and to labour under a complaint which baffled the fkill of the moft
eminent furgeons.

During this gloomy period his wife
was always abroad, or revelling with different men in the adjoining apartments
—indulging herfelf in every mode of extravagance, and totally unmindful of her
huf-

hufband's fituation or intereft. It was
natural at fuch a juncture to reflect on
his own folly in giving credit to her late
promifes of amendment, and to fuppofe
her capable of being ever actuated by the
principles of honour, fincerity, or truth.

Thefe reflections had their full force,
operated powerfully on the mind, and
encreafed the violence of his diftemper.
In his diftrefs and the extremity of dan-
ger, he fent for his landlady in the verge
of the court—complained heavily of his
wife—utter'd the moft bitter lamenta-
tions againft her undutiful behaviour—
and wifhed for death to terminate his
wretchednefs and afflictions.

However, his complaint at length
yielded to the powers of medicine, and
he

he began to gain a gradual share of bodily
health.—But the mind was still uneasy
and out of order—especially when he
saw the prodigalities of his wife, her ele-
gant wardrobe, and the many articles of
extravagance. Conscious that his circumstances could not afford such fantasti-
cal superfluities, and apprehensive they
must have been obtained by dishonoura-
ble means—he remonstrated on the oc-
casion, and against the many visitors that
came in pursuit of his wife and frequented his lodgings.

It was also seasonable to upbraid her of
unkindness and want of attention during
his severe illness—of wanton excursions
by day, and of absence from home for
whole nights. These remonstrances had
no effect—they made not the least im-
pression.

preffion. It is happy for the bulk of mankind, as well as for the peace of indi-viduals, that we do not meet with many inftances of fuch abandoned wives!

In behalf of this unfortunate hufband, it is alledged by all his early acquain-tance, that he was a fober, good-natured man, very tender and fond of his wife, and even partial to her levities.—But oppreffion and ill-ufage will render a wife man mad, and four the beft of tempers. Probably, this was his cafe at the time we mention—when a variety of domeftic grievances admitted of no alternative, but recourfe to liquors and intoxication. Hence frequent altercations with his wife at unfeafonable hours; and fometimes piftols were fired to the terror of the neighbourhood.

In

In ſhort, a ſerious ſkirmiſh at laſt happened at Cranſton's.   He in his own defence baſtinaded his wife ſeverely—ſhe
returned the compliment by ſwearing the
peace againſt her huſband.   Here a final
ſeparation took place — when he was
forced to fly into France, and ſhe to
change her quarters.

LETTER

LETTER XIV.

MADAM,

TO trace the windings of our heroine's
career, and follow her to every
place of elopement or intrigue, would
prove an endlefs as well as an infuperable
tafk. It would be to purfue a path terrifying in the commencement, impracticable in the profecution, and big with
deftruction in the end. However, we
have the beft authority to fay, that after
the final fkirmifh with her hufband in
Park Street, fhe was ufhered to Mrs.
Dodd's in Oxford Street, as a young
creature juft come from Wales, and totally unacquainted with the ways of the
town.

Women

Women are remarkable for invention, and feldom at a lofs how to form a tolerable excufe, and to palliate an aukward fituation. This pretext, however plaufible, did not long conceal her true character and connexions. The new landlady foon taxed her gueft of being the wife of an officer who lodged at Cranfton's, and fhe admitted the charge—acknowledged an elopement—urged in her own defence that her hufband had beat her feverely, and fhewed many bruifes on her arms.

Being now releafed from his controul, and at liberty to act unreftrained, the fyren allured a multitude of followers, and dealt her favours on the moft advantageous terms. When our heroine firft occupied thefe apartments, her finances

P were

were exceedingly low and fcanty; infomuch that the people of the houfe fupplied her neceffities with one fplendid
fhilling at a time. Even the milkman
was forced to fummon her to the court
of confcience for the contents of a trifling
bill.

The advantages of trade are precarious——but the perquifites of her avo-
cation were now confiderable, and the
fmiles of fortune feemed to preponderate
in her favour for a time. Hence fhe was
enabled at this period to keep a coach as
well as a chair occafionally; and though
the celebrated Lord D—— was the
oftenfible gallant, and who efcorted her
to many places public as well as private,
yet fhe carried on a correfpondence, and
had frequent interviews with feveral other
friends

friends behind the curtain. It can by no means be fuppofed that a woman of our heroine's paffions could prove faithful to a perfon of his Lordfhip's exhaufted finances and debilitated conftitution.

While fhe lodged at Cranfton's, and during her hufband's fevere illnefs, fhe had the art and dexterity to make exten-five connexions, and fome ufeful ones :— efpecially with that infamous pimp *Kildare,* who then kept a notorious houfe, in a court adjoining to Pall Mall. This mer-chant of female *chaftity,* was quite an adept in his profeffion; and paid the moft affiduous attention to the feveral ladies on his lift, at regular hours and places of appointment. It was at Grofvenor Gate, and generally between the hours of twelve and one, that he ufed to pay his

daily

daily attendance on our heroine, and to adjuſt the plan of meeting her cuſtomers in the evening at his own houſe or elſe-where

You alſo, madam, have ſome know-ledge of this faithful imp, and of the laws of his profeſſion. But your ac-quaintance, like a noxious planet, ſpreads ruin and contagion all around; even Mrs. Rudd was obliged to drop it at laſt. Our merchant had cauſe to repent that you ever frequented his houſe; for your preſence for a night occaſioned him a ſtagnation of trade, and almoſt the loſs of his life. When you waited there on fat *Lee* of the guards, and in the courſe of converſation gloried that you was a married woman, he inſtantly turned you out with indignation, and threatened

to

to run the mafter of the ceremonies through the body for introducing him to fuch unlawful game. An anecdote fomewhat fimilar muft not here be omitted.

It was a practice with our heroine, to write to perfonages whom fhe never faw, and to make overtures of intrigue and affignation. It unfortunately happened, that fhe once fent a card of this nature to an officer of the guards, and now on his deftination for America. Being ftartled at the contents, and totally unknown to the writer, he had the curiofity to make fome pertinent enquiries about fo extraordinary a character. The meffenger evaded an explanation as much as poffible; but at length was obliged to be communicative.

Matters

Matters were then concerted, that the wished for interview should take place. Accordingly, our heroine had immediate recourfe to drefs, and to all thofe arts and elegancies fo neceffary to render an ordinary figure, tolerable. Thus equiped, away she fallied for the place of appointment:—but alas! how poignant the mortification of being received in a formal manner, and not with the ardor of an impatient lover. In fhort, fhe met with a fevere lecture and fome chaftifement for her impudence, which diftreffed the texture of her delicate feelings extremely.

LETTER

L E T T E R XV.

M A D A M,

WHILE with pleasure we contemplate the character of a modest and amiable woman, yet it becomes a duty however painful the undertaking, to paint these abandoned *wives* in their true colours, and as a lesson of abhorrence to the rising generation. It is an attempt to guard the public from future deception, and to render honest service to our country.

A virtuous woman is an inestimable treasure, but one given to intrigue is the pest of society, as well as the ruin of individuals.—— Several of those unhappy

creatures

creatures of the town, and who are a nuisance to the streets, owe their misfortunes in a certain degree to an acquaintance with some of their own sex.—The following anecdote will illustrate the truth of these observations.

While our heroine lodged at Cranston's, an innocent young girl, fifteen years of age, was inveigled to carry errands to many places of infamous resort. In the execution of these commands, it was concerted that a person should watch this devoted victim and triumph over the spoils of innocence. One evening carrying a message to Kildare's, she was trepanned into a room, and by forcible means was——ruined.

Tremble, ye mothers, at the mention
of

of this horrid plot, and for the fate of your own innocent offspring!—Execrate the name of that unfeeling wretch, who could lend affiftance for the accomplifh-ment of fuch favage and inhuman deeds. Barbarous as this tranfaction certainly was, yet it is not the only one of the fort where-in our heroine has the credit of being concerned. One of the landlady's daugh-ters in Oxford Street, narrowly efcaped the fnare and a fimiliar cataftrophe.

But from thence our heroine was for-ced to make a precipitate retreat, and for fome years evaded the payment of a confiderable demand, and alfo the ex-pence of the carriages fhe kept. In the year 1772, when the noted Bolland of infamous memory was executed at Ty-burn for forgery, Mr. Ryder, mercer,

Q   called

'called on Mrs. Dodd, and acquainted
her that he had lately arrefted her old
lodger Mrs. Rudd, and under the name
of *Gore.*

It was obferved in a former letter,
that to trace the windings of our heroine's
career to every place of elopement or intrigue, would prove an endlefs and infuperable tafk.   Suffice it here to fay, that
Mrs. Dodd and her neighbours who
accommodated our heroine with the carriages, were paid their refpective demands by the unfortunate and infatuated
Daniel Perreau.

When forced to make a precipitate
retreat from Oxford Street, Mrs. Rudd
took fhelter at Mrs. Hufham's in Palace
Yard, Weftminfter, and continued there
for

for fome time —but here we muſt draw a vail—From thence, we follow her to Prince's Court, near Storey's Gate, where ſhe lived in no great affluence or ſplendour.

At this period, the advantages of her profeſſion were trifling ; and her finances ſo ſcanty, that ſhe was frequently heard to exclaim, If it was not for the goodneſs of good Lord Granby, who came to ſee her out of mere affection, ſhe muſt inevitably have ſtarved. One Lacey, a porter at Storey's Gate, was the perſon entruſted with errands at this juncture, and who carried many letters for her to an Alehouſe at Knightſbridge. But he declined now and then to execute her commands, and inſiſted on prompt payment.

She

She was once so destitute of money, and
all resources, as to give this man her
buckles to pawn, and which he did for
fifteen Shillings. And we shall see by
and bye, that this very man summoned
her to the court of conscience for twenty-
three shillings, and which she paid in a
week.

Several persons of suspicious appearance used to call on her at this place;
and the landlady not satisfied with the
conduct of her lodger, warned her out
on various accounts, and even suffered
her to go away considerably in her debt.
Our heroine was so bare of apparel at
this critical period, as to borrow a gown
of the servant of the house to carry her
to the new quarters, and where we shall
soon be obliged to follow her.

If

If this account fhould hurt a perfon of Mrs. Rudd's *fublimity of foul added to a refinement of fentiment,* we refer the curious to Mrs. *Wilfon,* the landlady fhe lodged with at this diftrefsful juncture.

LETTER

LETTER XVI.

MADAM,

TO delineate the adventures of fo eccentric a character as that of our heroine, it is neceffary to relate many difagreeable circumftances, and to vifit fome uncomfortable abodes.—She was now removed to the Coffee Houfe at Lambeth-marfh, and lodged in an airy apartment—a retreat where none but the loweft and pooreft proftitutes had recourfe for fhelter. Even Lacey the porter was here fhocked at the miferable fituation of his employer, when forced to repeat his vifits for the payment of humble and faithful fervices.

When

When a married woman forfeits the
moſt ſolemn engagement and the laws
of her protection, it is impoſſible to gueſs
what may be her cataſtrophe, or the ſum
of her diſtreſſes—To do juſtice to the
philoſophy of Mrs. Rudd, it is readily
allowed that ſhe has experienced the ex-
treams of good and ill fortune; has
known how to want as well as to abound.

Sometimes ſhe ſtrayed in Pleaſure's
ſofteſt path, and in ſcenes of voluptu-
ouſneſs ——had rich apparel, equipage,
jewels, and all the good things of this
world in abundance—But now ſhe was
deſtitute of friends and money, and without reputation. In ſuch a dilemma, her
ingenuity was employed in laying plans
of future eclat and enjoyment—every expedient

pedient was minutely canvaffed, and various projects fet on foot.

During a long courfe of intrigue, fhe
had made fome ufeful connexions, efpecially with a gang of the moft notorious
pimps. At this juncture, *one* of thefe
came to the dreary manfion, and gave
her hopes of better fcenes if fhe would
act a fpirited and a becoming part. For
this purpofe he relieved her prefent neceffities, charged her to be dexterous in
executing a fcheme, and doubted not
but fhe would foon get up in the world.

He then repaired to a young man in
the * Temple—affured him that he knew
of a fine girl at a boarding fchool that

was

* Mr. M———k.

was determined to elope—and believed that he could bring her to his chambers. But, fays the artful * pimp, a fuit of men's cloaths is abfolutely neceffary; a fuit of your's may anfwer the purpofe. Upon this a fuit of white and filver was procured, and Mifs foon made her appearance at the Temple—where fhe told an artful tale of getting over the garden wall, and of the many dangers fhe encounter'd to effect an elopement.

There is no doubt but that a woman, who could pafs for her own fifter, even in the arms of an accuftomed lover, had arts fufficient to impofe on this new gallant; and to perfuade how he triumphed over the fpoils of virtue. Hence, he fpared

R   no

* A—d—w White.

no expence to adorn the injured fair in proportion to her youth and perfonal charms;
and profperity feemed likely to be the portion of her better days. Being totally unacquainted with the irregularities of her
paft life, he foon expended a large fum,
and purchafed many fantaftical fuperflui-
ties for this paragon of confcious innocence. She now poffeffed an unbounded
influence in this perfon's circumftances
and affection, and fome profpect of an
advantage, which fhe never had before,
a certain independency.

Here we muft remark, that nature has
not been partial to our heroine's form,
and time has laid his heavy hand upon
her perfonal accomplifhments. But her
powers of pleafing in a certain degree,
have been well attefted by many martyrs;

and of *this* the numerous fons of Ifrael can bear an ample teftimony.

If her charms could lull fome modern Nabobs more powerfully than the opiates of the Eaft--if her own pale lips have affumed a temporary colour, which the new blown rofe might envy, yet they owe this appearance to the powers of art. If her teeth, which originally ftood in horizontal projection, appear now in white or even rows, yet this regularity is entirely owing to the file of the dentift. If gales, foft and inviting as the Arabian breeze, iffue from her breath, even thefe have been purchafed from the Perfumer's Shop.

Thus nature has not been partial to this extraordinary fyren, who has deftroy-

ed

ed the peace of many families, and has
proved the ruin of individuals. Her
benefactor in the Temple narrowly efcaped a fatal cataftrophe—but having avail-
ed herfelf of this acquaintance as much
as fhe could, fhe quitted that meridian
with perfect indifference, and travelled
weftward in fearch of frefh victims devoted to her fervice.

LETTER

LETTER XVII.

MADAM,

AIRS of addrefs, gentility and importance are diftinguifhing features
in our heroine's character; and it is allowed to her *credit*, that fhe is perfectly
acquainted with every fphere of life, and
never at a lofs how to behave in company of the peer or the porter. Notwithftanding the texture of her delicate feelings, yet fhe has more than once been
touched by very rough and unceremonious
hands. That hideous monfter, called a
fheriff's officer, has laid his dirty paws
on our heroine's tender frame. Many
difagreeable inftances of this nature have
occur'd to her ladyfhip.

It

It happened on a time, and what we forgot to mention in its proper place, that our heroine lodged at a certain houfe and on a prefumption of being a real lady of quality. The landlady never fufpect-ed her true character for a time, and till a confiderable fum for board and lodging was due—when fhe made bold to afk her ladyfhip for the whole or part of the debt. Our heroine was too well verfed in the ways of the world to be difconcerted at fo unfeafonable a demand; but with great compofure, airs of confe-quence, and eafy elegance, replied, that fhe was fomewhat furprized at the liberty of afking for fuch a trifle.

Upon this, fhe fummoned her foot-man, ordered him to haften to my Lord, and bring the money due to the landlady, infift-

infifting withal that his lordſhip would immediateiy ſend his chariot, being determined not to ſleep another night in the houſe of a landlady of ſuch indelicate manners and narrow principles.

The footman no doubt, underſtood her ladyſhip's meaning, and therefore knew how to conduct himſelf on the buſineſs, bowed obedience and retired. The landlady, during this plauſible ſcene, remained in a ſtate of ſuſpence—fearful ſhe had offended her ladyſhip if ſhe was a *real* lady, and who could not fail of being a deſirable lodger on punctual payment, and which then promiſed to be the caſe—the good woman made many apologies, pleaded poverty, and hoped her ladyſhip would not be affronted at the liberty occaſioned by her own neceſſitous circumſtances.

The

The footman being now returned, delivered the following card to his miftrefs, and which her ladyfhip with great condefcenfion defired the landlady to perufe. " My dear Lady, I muft beg ten thoufand pardons for not waiting on your ladyfhip before, but as I have been detained longer in the country than expected, hope you will excufe it. Am this moment going to court, and if I can get away in any time, will call at the banker's, and bring with me treble your fmall requeft. If I do not come this evening, I muft beg leave to pay my refpects to you in the morning."

This well concerted fcheme fucceeded. The landlady was convinced of her own rudenefs, as well as of her lodger's real confequence and importance—fully fatisfied

fied that fhe fhould receive a confiderable fum the next morning, the landlady retired to reft in good humour. But the next day brought neither Lord nor money; and this difappointment operated with redoubled force, awakened the landlady's fufpicions more than ever, and rendered her truly uneafy. And what alarmed her moft, was a difcovery, that the lady and footman had been earneftly employed great part of the day in packing up their own things, and probably more than they well could call their own. Having communicated her fufpicions to a neighbour, he prudently advifed her to have an officer in readinefs in the houfe for fear of fome iniquitous fcheme or plan of deception. The landlady purfued the advice, and planted an officer ready for execution if matters fhould turn out as there was

S   much

much room to fufpect. About midnight, and on a prefumption that the family was faft afleep, the footman was difpatched for a chair; and when her ladyfhip defcended, a perfon in waiting ordered the chairmen to fet down their fare, and feized upon her ladyfhip for further fecurity.

Her ladyfhip was then ufhered to a place by no means calculated for the reception of a perfon of delicate feelings; nor fuitable for the accommodation of a lady endowed with a fublimity of foul added to a refinement of fentiment. However, after a little confinement fhe found means to be fet at liberty: but this was not the only time that our heroine has been obliged to be complaifant to ill-looking myrmidons, and to put up with very difagreeable quarters.

LETTER

LETTER XVIII.

MADAM,

THE pimp who introduced our heroine to the Temple is a moſt extraordinary character, and perhaps has a more extenſive acquaintance with ladies of eaſy virtue than any other perſon in the kingdom. This merchant * had conſiderable buſineſs in his walk, and never deſerted his female cuſtomers in any ſituation, after he had once experienced their generoſity and affable demeanour. Our heroine had the dexterity to recommend herſelf to this perſon's notice and favour, ſoon after ſhe came upon the town; and he aſſumes the merit of rendering

* A—d—w W——

dering effential fervices, when Mrs. Rudd
was but little known in the fafhionable
world, or at places of genteel refort.

This trufty friend was firmly attached
to our heroine's intereft, whenever defert-
ed by an inconftant lover, or at a lofs for
fome frefh cull; and it is allowed that
there is no dirty jobb, but what this de-
teftable villian will undertake, in order
to promote his own intereft and diabolical purpofes. Confidering the great
number of women, married as well as
fingle, whom this fellow has feduced, it
is aftonifhing how he has fo long efcaped
that punifhment which his infamous profeffion fo juftly merits.

It was this artful pimp, this caterer
for the *voluptuous* and *libertines* of the
age,

age, that brought our heroine to several doating admirers ; particularly to a very respectable gentleman at the West end of the town, who for a while indulged her in every vanity, and permitted her to have plenty of rich cloaths and jewels in his name and on his credit. No doubt but an artful woman improved so glorious on opportunity, and made a proper use of such an enamoured dotard. It seems that she was peculiarly dexterous in making herself agreeable to enfeebled lovers; knew how to flatter, fondle and caress, and to exert all the craft of woman. Thus established in a splendid sphere, and surrounded with affluence, she was very bountiful to that benefactor who recommended her to so munificent a protector.

The

The pimp at this gay period, experienced great civilities and marks of uncommon genorofity; and the good natur'd lady would now and then liften to a private affignation, and condefcend to honour fome of his favourite cuftomers with a vifit. In this luftre and under thefe circumftances fhe lived for fome time, till the detection of an amorous interview between our heroine and a certain gallant broke off the connexion. This proved a fatal difcovery, an alarming ftroke to fo bountifnl a lady—fhe had now a gloomy profpect, by perceiving all her intereft loft in fo good a quarter. Her young lover had probably a greater flow of fpirits, but he was deftitute of thofe pecuniary confiderations fo neceffary to keep a woman above indigence and diftrefs; and being reduced to

a

a scanty pittance our heroine was forced to have recourse once more to her own ingenuity and the chapter of accidents.

However, the faithful pimp would not desert so generous a lady, or leave her in the day of adversity : but having planned a fresh scheme, he placed her for a time in a retired situation. Notwithstanding the great pains taken by the pimp, and the retirement of the place, yet it proved an inconvenient spot; for the real character of the lady being soon discovered, she was obliged to decamp rather abruptly, and old *Andrew* narrowly escaped with whole bones.

The lady's behaviour, and the fraud practised on the late cull at the temple, had roused the resentment of some lively youths,

youths, who were determined in their way
to have ample fatisfaction on fuch impu-
dent impoftors. Accordingly, they tra-
verfed the hundreds of Drury and all the
purlieus of Covent garden in fearch of
Andrew and his boarding-fchool girl;
but could by no means meet with the objects of their enquiry. At length they
ftumbled on the right fcent, and with full
refolution of being amply rewarded for
fo much trouble. The pimp and his
charge were apprized of the ftorm, and
made a precipitate retreat through a win-
dow; elfe the one would have *danced* in
the air, and the other have an opportunity of *fwimming* for life.

LETTER

LETTER XIX.

MADAM,

OLD *Andrew* and our heroine were put to their shifts, had not the courage to appear by day, and were forced to concert all their measures by night. Intervals of darkness corresponded in some degree with the office of the *one*, as well as with the duty of the *other*; and having no settled place of abode, our heroine was under a necessity of adopting precarious and temporary lodgings. The pimp from long services and experince had a kind of *right* to call on different customers, and even to disturb their rest and repose at unseasonable hours. It was his peculiar study to please per-

T   sons

fons of every complexion; to be ferviceable to mechanics, merchants, or
peers—to Jews as well as to Gentiles,
and to render his province as extenfively
ufeful as poffible.—He was no ftranger
in his vocation to the amorous fons of
Ifrael—who fometimes expend in *one* day
all the profits of the preceding week,
with fome artful female: and we have
the beft authority to affirm, that *Jews*
have lavifhed immenfe fums of money,
as well as the richeft jewels on our heroine, and in confideration of valuable
favours, for which no bill in equity could
be filed. It is a miftaken notion, that
peers and members of parliament are the
only perfons who deal in female charms,
or purchafe innocence in an illicit manner. The wealthy citizen has his country feat for particular purpofes, and the
whole

whole body of inferior merchants will imitate the conduct of thofe who have affluent fortunes to fupport their extravagance. An attachment to the charms of the fair fex, is by no means confined to thofe who bear the name of Chriftians —the Muffulmen and all the difciples of Mahomet, are confeffedly as fond of women as any people in Europe. And it is univerfally acknowledged, that the fons of Ifrael abound in riches, which greatly contribute to the gratification of unlawful pleafures, and brutal appetites. A child of Ifrael may not break the fab- bath, be he ever fo poor; yet no fooner does the fun fet on Saturday evening, but his confcience will permit him to break open an houfe in the city, and even commit murder in the environs of this metropolis.—If then a poor Ifraelite

who

who cries old clothes through the Streets of London, will commit felony, and even murder on *that* day, which the laws of this country have appropriated to the moft folmn purpofes—why may not the richer fort with equal propriety adjourn to the polite end of the town, to fpend, with *delicate* femᴁles, part of the money which by illicit practices they had procured the preceding week in the alley?

It is certain that our heroine became acquainted at this diftrefsful period with an amorous * Jew, and who will bear an interefting part in the enfuing volmue. It was the affiduity and attention of old *Andrew* the pimp that planned this connexion,

* S—v—e.

nection, and recommended our heroine
to the moft credulous lover that ever defcended from the race of Abraham.
This perfon, if report may be credited,
is of fuch an amorous difpofition, that
every woman was equally pleafing to
him, provided he had never feen her before. Variety is his darling paffion;
and it will appear in the profecution of
this narrative, that our heroine has paffed
with him for four different women. No
fooner was he introduced to Mrs. Rudd,
than he became extremely enamoured of
her charms, and he laid money at her
feet like the treafures of Ophir of old.
He never thought any expence too great,
fo as he could gratify his fenfual appetites.
and animal paffion. Had our heroine
been endowed with common prudence,
fhe might have made a good ufe of fo

plentiful

plentiful an harveft, and improved the
golden opportunity to fome purpofe.
But her prodigalities and diffipation were
boundlefs. A noted houfe in Leicefter
Fields for promifcuous reception, gave
the firft zeft to their amours, and laid
the foundation of that attachment which
effectually fleeced this amorous Ifraelite;
and in the long-run rendered him an object of poverty and contempt.

The indulgence of unlawful pleafures
or criminal purfuits, is generally attended
with the moft fatal and ruinous confe-
quences. Daily experience illuftrates the
truth of this affertion. The turbulence
of the paffions will admit of fome apology for the vivacity and irregularities of
youth; but to fee an old dotard with one
leg in the grave, lavifh of money as well

as prodigal of endearments on a common
proftitute, is truly fhameful and ridicu-
lous!--as to our heroine, fhe has no notion of any life but this. A fenfe of re-
ligion and a future ftate, have never entered into her creed; fhe therefore leads
a mere animal life, and like the beafts
that perifh, will infenfibly fink into ob-
fcurity.

END OF THE FIRST VOLUME.

www.ingramcontent.com/pod-product-compliance
Lightning Source LLC
Chambersburg PA
CBHW030851270326
41928CB00008B/1322